THE LOCH NESS MONSTER

THE

LOCH

NESS

MONSTER

An Easy-Read Fact Book

by
ELLEN RABINOWICH
Illustrated by
SALLY LAW

820536

FRANKLIN WATTS
New York/London 1979

Library of Congress Cataloging in Publication
Data

Rabinowich, Ellen
    The Loch Ness Monster.

    (An Easy-read fact book)
    Includes index.
    SUMMARY: Discusses the long search for the
Loch Ness Monster including the legends, eye-
witness accounts, underwater exploration of
Loch Ness, and photographs.
    1. Loch Ness Monster—Juvenile literature.
[1. Loch Ness Monster, 2. Monsters]
QL89.2.L6R3   001.9′44   78-21880
ISBN 0-531-02274-9

    R.L. 2.9 Spache Revised Formula

If you met a monster, what would you do?
Most people would probably scream and run,
but they would love to see a monster from a
distance. Monsters have fascinated people for
hundreds of years. Some people believe that
monsters are real. Others don't.

This book is about the most famous monster
in the world. Maybe it will help you decide
what to think about monsters.

Monsters are often thought of as big, frightening creatures that scientists can't explain. Some people think that prehistoric animals were monsters. These animals were giant reptiles that lived long before people. The dinosaur was one prehistoric animal.

A frightening monster in fairy tales is the dragon. In stories its sharp claws can tear a person to pieces, and its hot breath can burn a person to a crisp. However, scientists know that no real animal can breathe fire. The dragon is a make-believe monster.

For hundreds of years people all over the world have said they have seen real monsters. Some are thought to live in oceans and lakes. Others are said to haunt forests. Many children believe that monsters visit their bedrooms at night. These, of course, aren't real.

Sometimes monsters turn out to be real animals that we know. Long ago, many sailors were afraid of the sea. They were afraid that sea serpents or monsters would attack their ships. Sometimes, these monsters turned out to be strange, large animals like the octopus or giant squid. At other times, these monsters stayed a mystery.

One mysterious monster is so famous that it has often made newspaper headlines. Some people have left their jobs, homes, and families to look for this monster. Several British politicians thought this monster so important that they talked about it in Parliament. And three American astronauts asked to hear what these politicians were saying as their spaceship, the *Apollo 11,* raced toward the moon.

This monster has a name. It is called the Loch Ness Monster.

A tourist postcard about Nessie, the nickname of the Loch Ness Monster

Scientists about to use an eel cage to hunt for the monster

In the Scottish Highlands, there is a deep,
dark lake called Loch Ness. (Loch is the
Scottish word for "lake".) Tall pine trees
surround it, and on one shore the spooky ruins
of Urquhart Castle loom. There is something
very frightening about this lake. Thousands of
people say they have seen a monster rise out of
it.

The Scottish have given their famous Loch
Ness Monster a name. They call her Nessie.

What does Nessie look like? No one knows for sure. Some people say she has a long neck like a giraffe with small horns on her head. Others say that she has humps like a camel. Still others say she's over 40 feet (12 m) long, with flippers like a seal. Only on one point does everyone agree. Nessie doesn't look like anything they have ever seen.

People have also seen Nessie doing strange things. They say:

She streaks beneath the water like a
   torpedo.
She trails a sizzling wake of white foam.
She showers spray in all directions
   when she surfaces.
She sinks back into the water straight
   down like a stone.

Also, Nessie is not only a water monster! She has been spotted several times on land!

A photograph apparently showing Nessie's size in relation to the shore

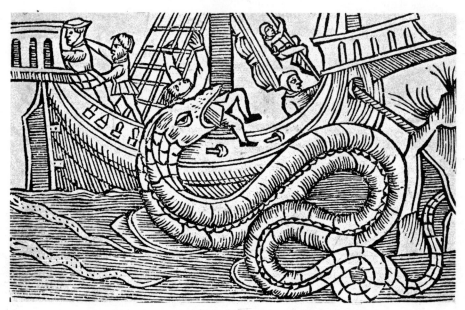

A sea serpent rather like the Loch Ness Monster in an old book of 1555

For years, there have been frightening stories about Nessie. Most people are just afraid when they see her. But sometimes Nessie makes people fear for their lives.

One story is about three fishermen. Late one night they set out in a small boat looking for salmon. Loch Ness is a fine lake for fishing. It is full of salmon, eel, pike, and trout. But these fishermen were breaking the law. No fishing is allowed in Loch Ness after eight at night.

It was a beautiful spring night. The men
were sure they would catch lots of fish.
Suddenly, they forgot about fishing. Something
very big was under their boat. And that
something was lifting them up and out of the
water. The men went white with fright. What
strange force could do this? Then, suddenly

their boat came back down. The men saw a giant shape swim away. Was it Nessie? The men didn't know. But they did know they would never break the law again.

Could Nessie really be a monster? Are such creatures real? One Dutch scientist, Dr. Bernard Heuvelmans, says "Yes." Dr. Heuvelmans is different from most scientists. He believes that the giant creatures called sea serpents that frightened sailors were, in fact, real and he believes Nessie is one of them.

Some scientists believe that Nessie isn't a monster at all. They think she might be some kind of mammal that we know about, like the sea cow or otter. Near Alaska, one kind of sea cow grew to 35 feet (10.6 m).

However, other scientists believe differently. They are sure that this giant kind of sea cow died out years ago. Also, sea cows don't have long necks like Nessie and must surface to breathe. If Nessie breathed air like other mammals, she would probably be seen more often.

A sea cow

Could Nessie be a prehistoric animal like the dinosaur? These animals are believed to have died out long ago. But many people who have seen Nessie are then asked to look at pictures of prehistoric animals. They are also asked which one she looks like. Most pick the same one — the **plesiosaur** (PLEE-see-a-sore).

The plesiosaur was a giant reptile that lived millions of years ago. It had a long neck, a fat body, and a long tail. It also had small flippers like a seal.

23

Scientists know that plesiosaurs once lived near Loch Ness. However, plesiosaurs are believed to have died out 70 million years ago.

Some ideas about Nessie come from legends. One tells about a very big creature called the

Great Orm. Drawings of it have been found on stones near Loch Ness. Some people believe this legend. They think Nessie is a huge worm.

A worm is an **invertebrate** (in-VERT-uh-bret), an animal without bones. If Nessie is a worm, that explains why none of her ancestors' bones were ever found.

However, scientists don't know of any worms that are as long or wide as Nessie is said to be.

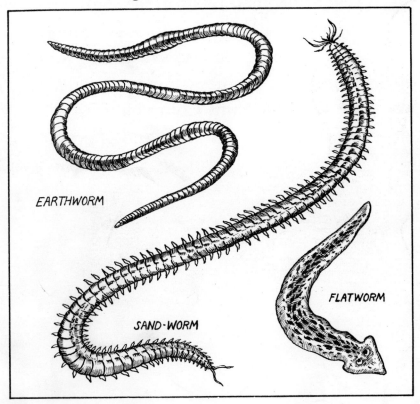

EARTHWORM

SAND-WORM

FLATWORM

In the sixth century, a holy man named Saint Columba came to Loch Ness. To him, Nessie was a frightening "Water monster."

The story goes like this. Saint Columba asked one of his men to swim across the lake and bring back a boat. Soon the swimmer heard a great roar. He also saw a big, wide-open mouth. The poor swimmer thought he was done for. But Saint Columba was watching. He raised his arms and cried out to the monster with holy words. And the monster was driven away.

No one can be quite sure if this story about Saint Columba and the monster really happened. But it was the first story about this monster ever written down. It was called "Of the Driving Away of a Certain Water Monster by Virtue of Prayer."

Also at another time, when the blessed man was for a number of days in the province of the Picts, he had to cross the river Nes [Ness]. When he reached its bank, he saw a poor fellow being buried by other inhabitants; and the buriers said that, while swimming not long before, he had been seized and most savagely bitten by a water beast. Some men, going to his rescue in a wooden boat, though too late, had put out hooks and caught hold of his wretched corpse. When the blessed man heard this, he ordered notwithstanding that one of his companions should swim out and bring back to him, by sailing, a boat that stood on the opposite bank. Hearing this order of the holy and memorable man, Lugne mocu-Min obeyed without delay, and putting off his clothes, excepting his tunic, plunged into the water. But the monster, whose appetite had earlier been not so much sated as whetted for prey, lurked in the depth of the river. Feeling the water above disturbed by Lugne's swimming, it suddenly swam up to the surface, and with gaping mouth and with great roaring rushed towards the man swimming in the middle of the stream. While all that were there,

This story also raised a big question. If Saint Columba spotted Nessie in the sixth century, is she thousands of years old today? Absolutely not! Not even monsters can live that long. If Nessie is real, she must be the great-great-great-grandchild of the first one.

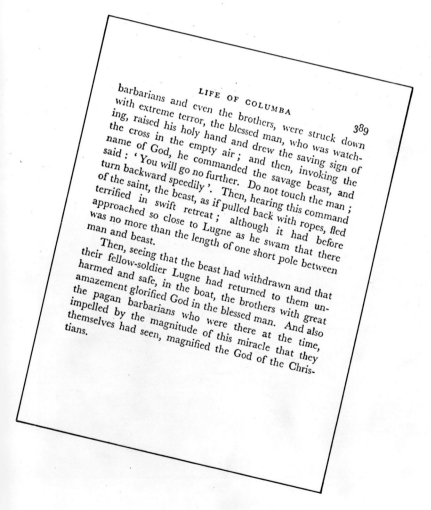

LIFE OF COLUMBA   389

barbarians and even the brothers, were struck down with extreme terror, the blessed man, who was watching, raised his holy hand and drew the saving sign of the cross in the empty air; and then, invoking the name of God, he commanded the savage beast, and said: 'You will go no further. Do not touch the man; turn backward speedily'. Then, hearing this command of the saint, the beast, as if pulled back with ropes, fled terrified in swift retreat; although it had before approached so close to Lugne as he swam that there was no more than the length of one short pole between man and beast.

Then, seeing that the beast had withdrawn and that their fellow-soldier Lugne had returned to them unharmed and safe, in the boat, the brothers with great amazement glorified God in the blessed man. And also the pagan barbarians who were there at the time, impelled by the magnitude of this miracle that they themselves had seen, magnified the God of the Christians.

But how did Nessie's ancestors get into Loch Ness in the first place? Only one little river joins Loch Ness to the sea. Nessie is said to be too big to swim through this river.

Several geologists explained it this way. Thousands of years ago there was no Loch

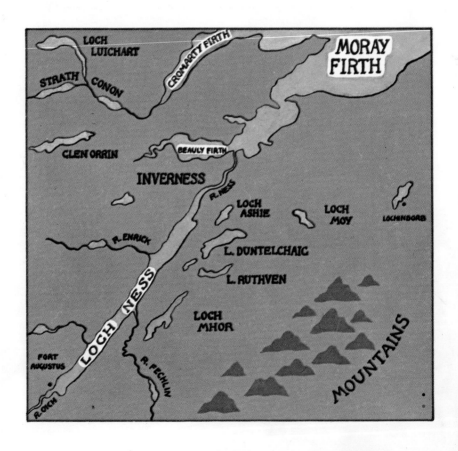

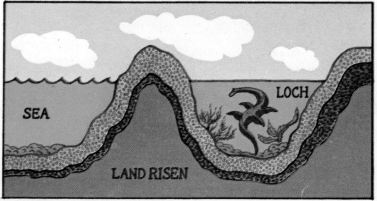

Ness. This lake was really part of the sea. The Ice Age helped change all this. Land rose between certain areas of water, making lakes.

Possibly Nessie's ancestors were trapped in Loch Ness after this happened.

Seals are mammals — and some people think the Loch Ness Monster could be a giant seal or an otter

For years, Nessie has puzzled scientists. Was she a mammal? A plesiosaur? Was she anything at all? Today, scientists still are not sure. Most say there is not enough information to prove she is real.

However, sometimes there are animals alive that scientists don't know about. For years, scientists were sure that a prehistoric fish called the **coelacanth** (SEE-la-kanth) was no longer alive. Then, one was found swimming in the Indian Ocean. Perhaps Nessie is like this prehistoric fish. Perhaps she is an animal long thought dead, but alive and well today.

A coelacanth

No one will be sure what Nessie is until she is found or caught. However, looking for Nessie takes a lot of work. Loch Ness is very deep and dark. There are hardly any beaches, and in some places the water is over 900 feet (274 m) deep.

Scientists preparing equipment to hunt the Loch Ness Monster

View of Loch Ness — with a shadow in the right foreground...a fish, a wave ...or the Monster?

Loch Ness is also filled with rotting plant material called peat. This turns the water dark brown like coffee. Divers who look for Nessie are always disappointed. They can't see anything.

Most of the world never heard of Nessie until 1933. Then people began building a road alongside Loch Ness. Before then, hardly anyone went there. Now loads of people pass by every day. Perhaps Nessie wanted to know what all their noise was about. Whatever the reason, loads of people began seeing a monster.

Surveying Loch Ness in 1933

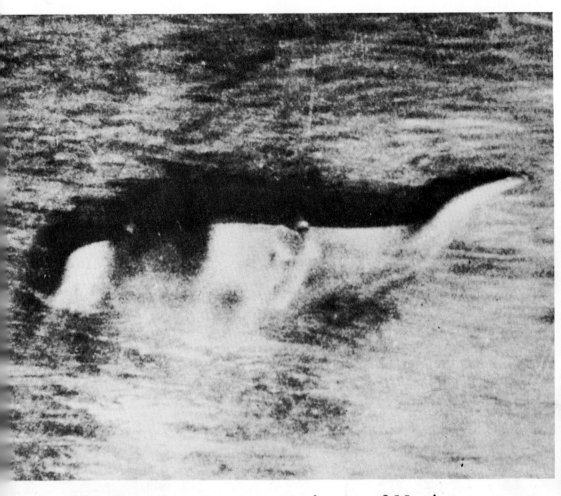

The first person to snap a picture of Nessie was a Scottish Highlander named Hugh Gray. The picture was very fuzzy, but a Scottish newspaper printed it anyway. The photograph made people very excited. Everyone wanted to know more about the monster.

Soon a big newspaperman from England came to Loch Ness. He brought along a game hunter and a photographer. Monster stories sell loads of newspapers. Shortly, the hunter found giant footprints by the shore. Everyone was very happy. Nessie had not been spotted on land before. A plaster cast was made and rushed to the British Museum.

The newspaperman was too excited to wait for the museum's answer. He ran a big story about Nessie right away. He should have

waited. The museum found something very strange. The footprints had been made by a stuffed hippopotamus's foot. For a while, the world had been fooled by the hunter's trick.

Since 1934, thousands of people have reported seeing Nessie. To these people, Nessie isn't a trick. She is very real. Some people have even photographed her. None of these photographs are very clear, and they all look different.

Searching for the Monster in a mini-submarine

One shows a huge body and a very long neck. It is called the Surgeon's Photograph because a doctor took it. Many believe it is Nessie's best picture. It also looks very much like a plesiosaur.

Other photographs show this:

Three humps rising out of the lake. They are all the same size.

Two humps. One is bigger than the other. One hump.

No humps. Just a V-shaped wake.

Could any of these be Nessie? Today, scientists still are not sure.

43

In time, so many people became interested in Nessie that in 1962 the Loch Ness Phenomena Investigation Bureau was formed, headed by a member of the British Parliament, David James. At first, Mr James didn't believe in Nessie. Today people from his bureau spend many hours looking for her.

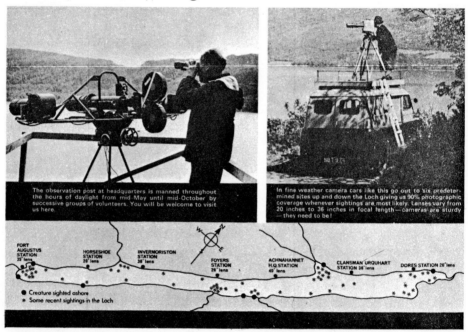

The observation post at headquarters is manned throughout the hours of daylight from mid-May until mid-October by successive groups of volunteers. You will be welcome to visit us here.

In fine weather camera cars like this go out to six predetermined sites up and down the Loch giving us 90% photographic coverage whenever sightings are most likely. Lenses vary from 20 inches to 36 inches in focal length—cameras are sturdy —they need to be!

● Creature sighted ashore
✳ Some recent sightings in the Loch

Part of a poster showing the Bureau's work

Several newspapers and universities have also joined the search. Every summer, teams of scientists travel to Loch Ness for a scientific monster hunt. These expeditions use special equipment like **sonar** (SO-nar) and underwater cameras. Sonar is a way of using electronics to discover the size, depth, and movement of an object.

Unfortunately, sonar isn't perfect. Once, scientists were sure they had found Nessie. However, their monster turned out to be a large shoal of fish.

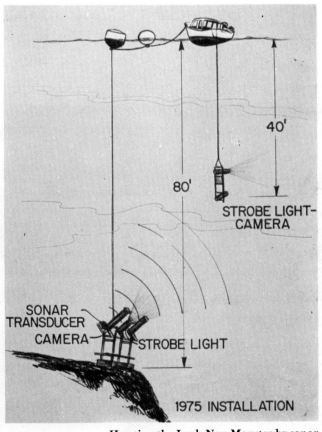

Hunting the Loch Ness Monster by sonar

The real star of one expedition was the underwater camera. In 1975, a member of the Boston Academy of Applied Sciences took two photographs with it that could have been Nessie. One looked like a dragon's head with horns. The other looked like the body of a plesiosaur. Which one was Nessie? Both or neither? Again, the photographs were not clear enough for scientists to be sure. However, the British

The dragon's head photograph

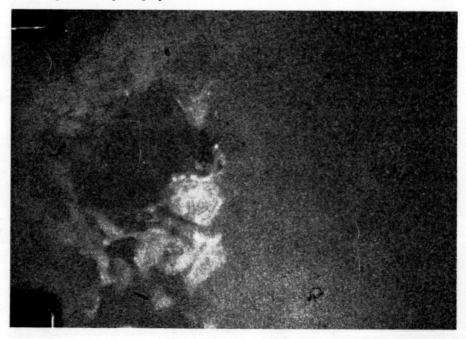

naturalist, Sir Peter Scott, was so sure the
pictures were genuine that he gave Nessie a
scientific Latin name: *Nessitara rhombopteryx*.

Today, thousands of people go to Loch Ness.
Some spend hours staring at the lake through
their hotel windows. Others stand all day by its
shore. And still others ride around in small
boats. All these people want one thing: to see
the world's most famous monster — NESSIE.

The plesiosaur photograph

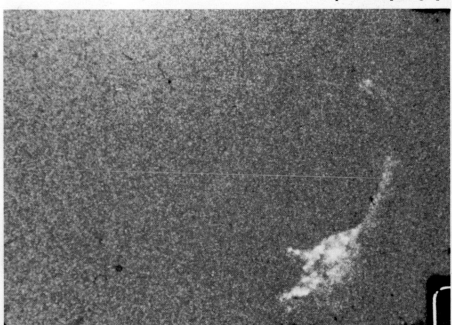

INDEX

Thanks are due to the following for kind permission to reproduce photographs:
Associated Newspapers Ltd., Courtesy of the London *Daily Mail* (p.41); Bettmann Archive (p.16); Janet and Colin Bord (p.24); British Natural History Museum (p.33); Brown Brothers (p.20); Field Enterprises Educational Corporation of Chicago (p.40); Fortean Picture Library (p.5 bottom); Loch Ness Phenomena Bureau (p.44); P. A. MacNab (p.14); New York Public Library Picture Collection (p.5 top, p.10); Popperfoto (p.32, p.36, p.42, p.43 bottom); Dr. Rines/Syndication International (p.46, p.47); *Scottish Daily Record and Sunday Mail* (p.37); Scottish Tourist Board (p.12); *Sunday Express* (p.43 top); Syndication International (p.34); United Press International (p.11, p.35)